1922

Five nations send athletes to Paris, France, to compete in the first of four Women's Olympics.

1924

The First Winter Olympic Games are held in Chamonix, France. Later in the year, the Eighth Summer Olympics are held in Paris.

U.S. golfer Glenna Collett wins 59 of the 60 matches she plays this year.

TRUDY'S BIG SWIM

How Gertrude Ederle Swam
the English Channel
and Took the World by Storm

by SUE MACY
Illustrated by MATT COLLINS

HOLIDAY HOUSE ● NEW YORK

WIND buffeted the tugboat *Alsace*
in the rough waters of the English Channel.
With each gust, the men and women on board
steadied themselves before looking anxiously at the churning sea.
They scanned the surface and did not relax
until they spied a blur of red moving rhythmically through the waves.
Gertrude Ederle, in her cheerful swimming cap, was still going strong.

At 7:09 that morning, Gertrude—or Trudy—
had waded into the surf from a beach in France.
Her goal was to swim all the way to England
by crossing the waterway between them,
the English Channel, at its narrowest point.

The distance measured about 21 miles on a map,
but no one could swim across the Channel in a straight line.
Changing tides and swift currents threw swimmers off course,
adding many miles to the journey.

Two hundred people had tried to swim the Channel before.
Only five men had made it, and none on their first try.
They had to overcome violent storms, numbing cold, exhaustion,
leg cramps, painful jellyfish stings and ongoing fears about sharks.
Trudy's trainer, Bill Burgess, had failed twelve times before
succeeding.

Now Trudy wanted to be the first woman to conquer the Channel. "England or drown is my motto," she had told reporters the day before. "I could never face people at home again unless I had got across."

Trudy was still smarting over her failed Channel attempt
the previous August.
She was not used to failure.
At a time when female athletes were finally starting to
make headlines on the sports page, the *New York Times*
had called Trudy "the greatest free style swimmer of her
sex ever developed."

She had burst onto the swimming scene as a teenager in 1922,
setting records in six different sprint distances in one day.
In 1924, she earned one gold and two bronze medals at the Olympics.
By 1925, Trudy had set 29 records in events
as short as 50 yards and as long as half a mile.
That year, she also proved she could conquer longer distances,
finishing a 22-mile swim from her hometown of New York City
to Sandy Hook, New Jersey, in seven hours and eleven minutes.

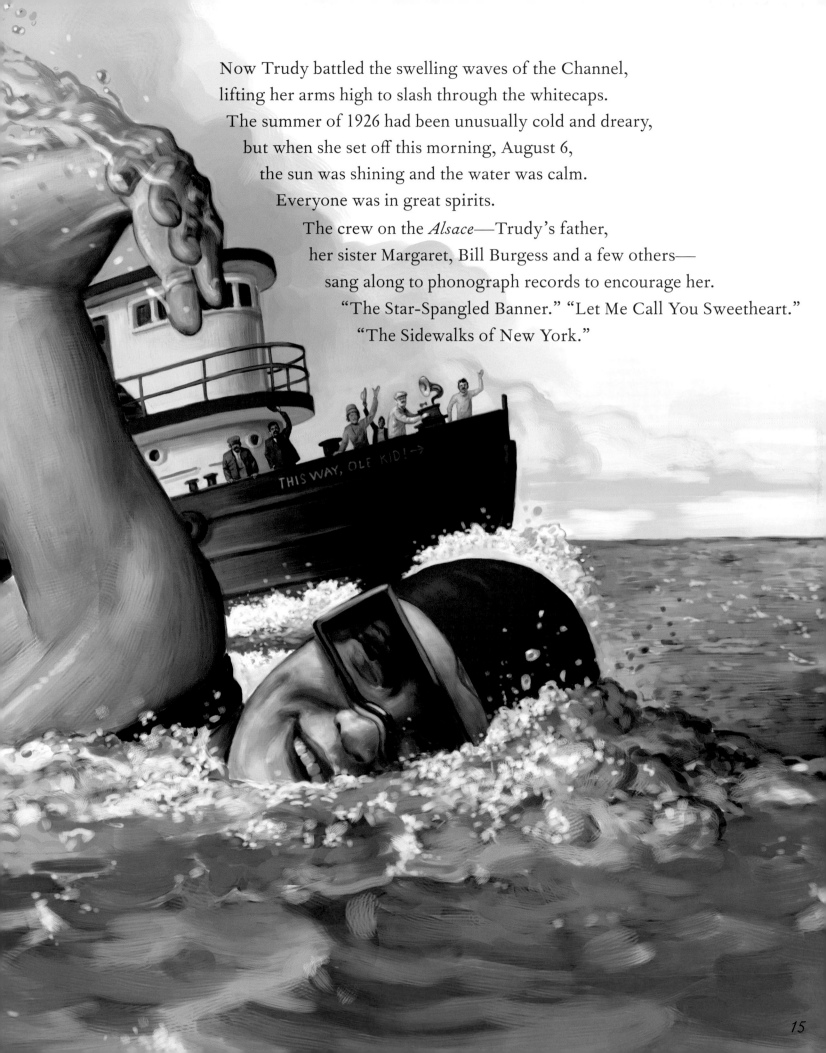

Now Trudy battled the swelling waves of the Channel,
lifting her arms high to slash through the whitecaps.
The summer of 1926 had been unusually cold and dreary,
but when she set off this morning, August 6,
the sun was shining and the water was calm.
Everyone was in great spirits.
The crew on the *Alsace*—Trudy's father,
her sister Margaret, Bill Burgess and a few others—
sang along to phonograph records to encourage her.
"The Star-Spangled Banner." "Let Me Call You Sweetheart."
"The Sidewalks of New York."

THIS WAY, OLE KID! →

Trudy swam to the rhythm of the songs
and joined in during breaks to rest and eat.
The rules forbade Channel swimmers from touching boats or
other people during their crossings, so food
was delivered from the *Alsace* in a net at the end of a pole.
Trudy treaded water as she drank chicken broth from a baby bottle
and gnawed on a leg of fried chicken.

But around noon, while Trudy was eating,
the wind picked up and the water became choppy.
Conditions only got worse as the afternoon wore on.
Trudy had to dodge chunks of driftwood stirred up by the current,
along with slimy, poisonous jellyfish hurled at her by the waves.

By six p.m., Bill Burgess began to fear that
she would be injured if she kept swimming.
Others aboard the *Alsace* grew worried, too.
Finally someone shouted, "Come on, girl, come out!"
But Trudy, who was as determined as ever to finish,
yelled back, "What for?"
Her response set off a round of cheers.

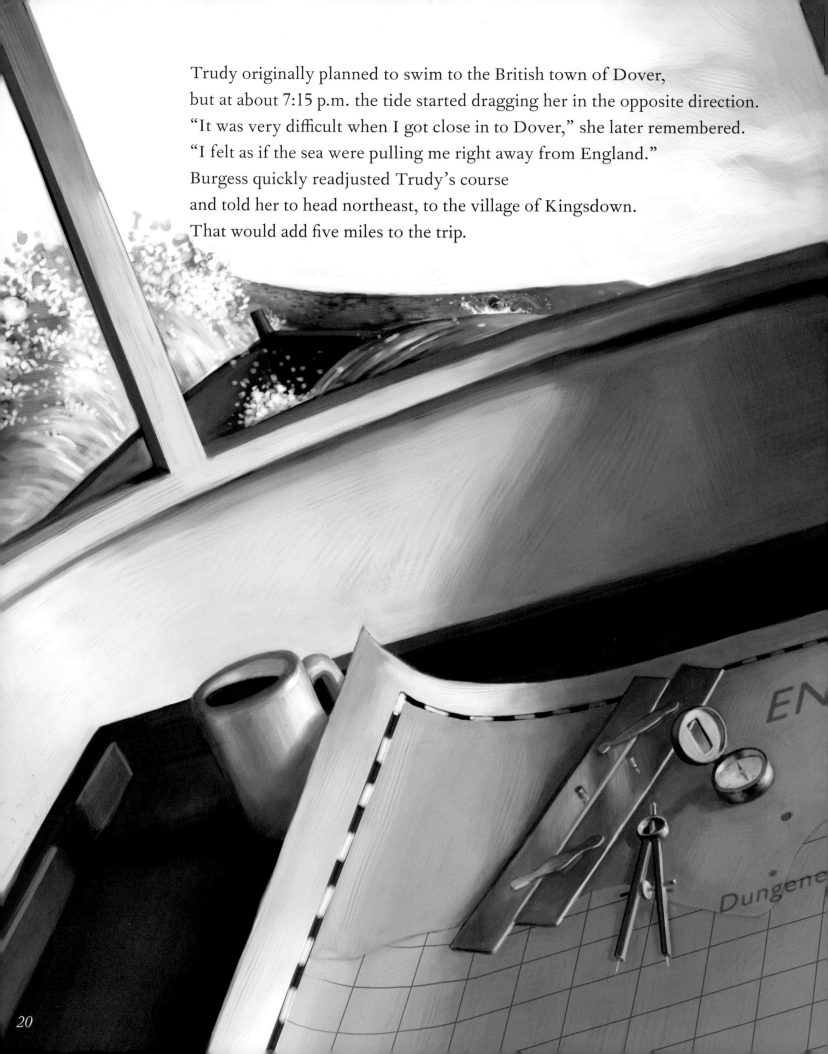

Trudy originally planned to swim to the British town of Dover,
but at about 7:15 p.m. the tide started dragging her in the opposite direction.
"It was very difficult when I got close in to Dover," she later remembered.
"I felt as if the sea were pulling me right away from England."
Burgess quickly readjusted Trudy's course
and told her to head northeast, to the village of Kingsdown.
That would add five miles to the trip.

Despite the setback, Trudy continued swimming.
By now she had been in the water more than 12 hours.
The coats of grease she had slathered on her body
to keep warm had worn off.
She was freezing, and so very tired.
As the sky grew dark, Trudy began to wonder
if she would fail to accomplish her goal again.
She called out to the *Alsace* to ask if the crew thought she could make it.
"Assured!" they yelled back.
They were certain she could.

THIS WAY, OLE KID! →

Not long after that Trudy began to see bursts
of red and green in the distance.
News of her approach had spread
along the coast north of Dover and
thousands of people had come out to greet her,
lighting bonfires and colorful flares.

Those with automobiles directed their headlights
out to sea. A searchlight scanned the water,
settling on the *Alsace* and the lone figure
who propelled herself through the
waves below.

That figure continued to draw closer until finally, at 9:48 p.m.,
Gertrude Ederle rose out of the water and stood
on the English shore, just north of Kingsdown beach.
She had crossed the Channel in 14 hours and 39 minutes.
Not only was she the first woman to complete the swim;
she also beat the record of the fastest man by close to two hours.

After spending so long in a cocoon of water,
Trudy needed a moment to adjust to solid ground.
But swarms of well-wishers descended on her,
reaching out to shake her hand or pat her on the back.
Trudy started to panic and was relieved when
her father and sister came on shore and directed her to a rowboat.
She climbed in quickly and returned to the quiet calm of the *Alsace*.

As the *Alsace* headed to Dover, newspapers around the
world rewrote the lead stories for their next editions.
"THE CHANNEL CONQUERED BY A GIRL,"
screamed the front page of a British daily.
"One of the greatest athletic achievements of all time,"
declared a German tabloid.
Trudy left it to others to consider the meaning of her success.
She made her way to Dover's Grand Hotel,
where she scarfed down four ham sandwiches
and some juicy, fresh tomatoes.
Then she took a long, hot bath
and crawled into bed for a well-earned rest.

AFTERWORD

Gertrude Ederle's English Channel swim was one of the defining moments in women's sports history. It also was an indicator of a sea change in the lives of American women. In 1920, the 19th Amendment became part of the U.S. Constitution, granting women the right to vote in all elections. With that came their increased involvement in many aspects of public life, including sports. Americans embraced sports as both spectators and participants in the 1920s, and newspaper sports pages grew into sports sections to satisfy their interest. Women's athletic achievements were widely reported in those sections, becoming visible evidence of their expanding place in American society. Even the *Woman Citizen*, a former suffrage magazine that became the official publication of the League of Women Voters, appreciated the impact of sports. "Nothing in the world more strikingly marks the great gap between the girl of today and her grandmother than that girl's place in the world of sport," reported one article in 1925.

When it came to swimming, relaxed standards of dress for women opened up new possibilities. Early in the 20th century, it was typical for women who wanted to take a dip to wear heavy, bulky bathing costumes that covered them from the neck to the knees, along with stockings, bathing slippers and caps. Trudy never could have lasted 14 hours in the English Channel weighed down by those clothes. Fortunately, the new freedoms of the 1920s made it acceptable for her to wear a two-piece bathing suit that was not so different from those some women wear today.

Distance swimming was all the rage in the 1920s, and no challenge was greater than the English Channel. Two days before Trudy succeeded, a reporter for the *New York Sun* tried to explain why people took on this nearly impossible task. He wrote that the Channel satisfied a human being's urge "to pit his puny strength against the cosmic forces of nature." In 1926 alone, more than a dozen men and women flocked to France and England to attempt a Channel swim. In the weeks after Trudy's triumph, one woman, Amelia "Mille" Gade Corson, and one man, Ernst Vierkoetter, also made it across. Corson was the first mother to swim the English Channel and Vierkoetter set a new speed record of 12 hours, 38 minutes.

Trudy was cheered by two million people at a tickertape parade when she returned home to New York City in late August. But sadly, she soon experienced a series of setbacks. Trudy was a shy young woman who had been living with a hearing problem since she had the measles as a child. She was overwhelmed by her sudden fame and the demands of the public appearances that went with it. After the swim—possibly in part *because* of it—her hearing continued to decline until she was totally deaf by age 22. A few years later, she took a terrible fall and severely injured her back. Although doctors told her she might never be able to walk or swim again, Trudy proved them wrong. Marshaling the same strength she had used to defeat the Channel, she regained her mobility and dedicated herself to teaching deaf children how to swim. She lived into the next century and died on November 30, 2003, at age 98.

AUTHOR'S NOTE

If you do any research on Gertrude Ederle's life, you're likely to find many sources that say she was born in 1906, and she was 19 years old when she swam the English Channel. These sources are wrong. Trudy was born October 23, 1905, and she was 20 when she swam the Channel. Her gravestone at Woodlawn Cemetery in the Bronx, New York, confirms her age, as does the book *America's Girl: The Incredible Story of How Swimmer Gertrude Ederle Changed the Nation*, cowritten by her niece, Mary Ederle Ward. That book suggests Trudy went along with the misconception about her birth year because swimming the Channel as a teenager seemed more impressive than swimming it as a 20-year-old.

SOURCES AND RESOURCES

Contemporary newspaper accounts of Gertrude Ederle's 1926 swim are colored by the fact that the whole effort was sponsored by the *New York Daily News*. Reporter Julia Harpman was with Trudy the entire time she trained at Cape Gris Nez, France, delivering detailed chronicles of her preparations, and Trudy herself wrote frequent columns in the *Daily News* during that time. The editors discouraged Trudy from speaking to journalists from other newspapers, and Harpman made sure she was the only reporter on the *Alsace* during the swim. Other papers did cover the event, with the *New York Times* doing a particularly good job, but only Harpman had the inside track. So anyone interested in reading newspaper accounts of Trudy's swim would do well to start with the *Daily News*.

Here are some other sources about Trudy and her "Big Swim."

BOOKS

America's Girl: The Incredible Story of How Swimmer Gertrude Ederle Changed the Nation by Tim Dahlberg with Mary Ederle Ward and Brenda Greene (New York: St. Martin's Press, 2009). With the swimmer's niece as one of the authors, this adult book offers a unique perspective on Trudy's story.

The Great Swim by Gavin Mortimer (New York: Walker & Company, 2008). This well-researched, adult account of the numerous men and women who raced to be the first to swim the English Channel in 1926 is as engaging as it is informative. It provides excellent perspective on Trudy's accomplishment.

FILM CLIP

News in Brief, A Universal International News report from August 27, 1959, this short film looks back at Trudy's swim and the tickertape parade that followed it. www.youtube.com/watch?v=84fYnCEVfJI

WEBSITES

Gertrude Ederle Biography
www.biography.com/people/gertrude-ederle-9284131

The Biography.com website presents an accessible summary of Trudy's life and accomplishments.

Queen of the Channel: Gertrude Ederle, 1926–1953
www.queenofthechannel.com/gertrude-ederle

This compilation of articles and reviews of books about Trudy on the website of the Channel Swimming Association also features links to information about other women who held the title of fastest female Channel swimmer over the years.

SOURCE NOTES

Pages

10–11 "failed twelve times": "Burgess of Davenham: Thomas William Burgess," www.derbyburgess.ca/histories/twburgess.php, accessed May 11, 2015. Other sources state that Burgess made it on his 11th or 14th try.

"England or drown . . . across": *Boston Post*, August 6, 1926, quoted in *The Great Swim* by Gavin Mortimer, New York, Walker & Company, 2008, p. 130.

12–13 "the greatest free style . . . ": "Predict Victory for Miss Ederle," *New York Times*, June 14, 1925.

"29 records": International Swimming Hall of Fame: Honorees: Gertrude Ederle (USA), www.ishof.org/gertrude-ederle-(usa).html, accessed April 17, 2015.

19 "Come on, girl, come out!": *The Great Swim*, p. 149.

"What for?": "Hour by Hour With Ederle in Epic Swim," by Julia Harpman, *New York Daily News*, August 7, 1926, p. 4.

20 "It was very . . . England": *Herald Tribune*, August 8, 1926, quoted in *The Great Swim*, p. 153.

23 "Assured": "Wins After Trainer Loses Hope in Howling Gale," by Julia Harpman, *New York Daily News*, August 7, 1926, p. 7.

26 Original reports cited Trudy's time as 14 hours and 31 minutes (in the *New York Times*) and 14 hours and 34 minutes (in the *New York Daily News*). However, the Channel Swimming Association, established in 1927 to authenticate Channel swims, lists Trudy's time at 14 hours, 39 minutes.

31 "THE CHANNEL . . . ": Quoted from the *Daily Sketch* in *America's Girl: The Incredible Story of How Swimmer Gertrude Ederle Changed the Nation*, by Tim Dahlberg, New York, St. Martin's Press, 2009, p. 144.

"One of the greatest . . . ": Quoted from the *Berliner Nachtausgabe* in *America's Girl*, p. 144.

32 "Nothing in the world . . . world of sport": "How Weak Is the Weaker Sex?" *Woman Citizen*, September 1925, p. 15, quoted in "Icons of Liberty or Objects of Desire? American Women Olympians and the Politics of Consumption," by Mark Dyerson, *Journal of Contemporary History*, July 2003, p. 437.

"to pit . . . of nature": George Trevor, *New York Sun*, August 4, 1926, quoted in *The Great Swim*, p. 124.

ACKNOWLEDGMENTS

I love to swim and I love to write about women athletes, so Gertrude Ederle's triumph over the English Channel has always inspired me on both a personal and a professional level. When Kelly Loughman and Mary Cash at Holiday House suggested that I write a picture book about Trudy's swim, I embraced the challenge. It's been a joy to revisit this iconic moment in sports history.

So thanks to Kelly and Mary and everyone else at Holiday House. Thanks, also, to Matt Collins for once again being a wonderful collaborator, and to my personal support team—you know who you are. As I wrote this book, I thought often of one of my sports idols, marathon swimmer Diana Nyad, who topped off a brilliant career in 2013 by swimming from Cuba to Florida at age 64. One of my coolest memories took place some 20 years ago, when, at a conference in Dallas, she and I swam laps together.

For Diana Nyad, a Trudy for our time, and then some—S.M.
To Jason, my beamish boy—M.C.

Text copyright © 2017 by Sue Macy
Art copyright © 2017 by Matt Collins
All Rights Reserved
HOLIDAY HOUSE is registered in the U.S. Patent and Trademark Office.
Printed and Bound in November 2016 at Toppan Leefung, DongGuan City, China.
The artwork was created with Prismacolor pencils, Denril vellum, Painter 12 and Adobe Photoshop.

Above photo of Trudy, Library of Congress, Prints & Photographs Division, LC-DIG-ggbain-37118
www.holidayhouse.com
First Edition
1 3 5 7 9 10 8 6 4 2

Library of Congress Cataloging-in-Publication Data

Names: Macy, Sue. | Collins, Matt, illustrator.
Title: Trudy's big swim : how Gertrude Ederle swam the English Channel and
took the world by storm / by Sue Macy ; illustrated by Matt Collins.
Description: First edition. | New York : Holiday House, [2017]
Identifiers: LCCN 2016003168 | ISBN 9780823436651 (hardcover)
Subjects: LCSH: Ederle, Gertrude, 1906—Juvenile literature. |
Swimmers—United States—Biography—Juvenile literature. | Women
Swimmers—United States—Biography—Juvenile literature.
Classification: LCC GV838.E34 M34 2017 | DDC 792.2/1092 [B]—dc23
LC record available at https://lccn.loc.gov/2016003168

TIME LINE OF 1920s SPORTS HIGHLIGHTS
(CONT.)

1926

Suzanne Lenglen of France beats Helen Wills of the U.S., 6–3, 8–6, in the only match ever between these two international tennis stars.

Gertrude Ederle becomes the first woman to swim across the English Channel.

Eight countries participate in the Women's World Games (formerly the Women's Olympics) in Göteborg, Sweden.

Pitcher Satchel Paige begins his professional baseball career with the Chattanooga Black Lookouts of the Negro Southern League.

1927

The Harlem Globetrotters play their first basketball game.

The U.S. beats England in the first Ryder Cup golf challenge.